Contents

Lessons of Maplin

IS THE MACHINERY
FOR GOVERNMENTAL DECISION-MAKING
AT FAULT?

CHRISTOPHER FOSTER
Director, Centre for Urban Economics, LSE

J. B. HEATH
Professor of Economics, London Graduate School of Business Studies

G. H. PETERS
Brunner Professor of Economic Science, University of Liverpool

J. E. FFOWCS WILLIAMS
Rank Professor of Engineering (Acoustics), University of Cambridge

SIR PETER MASEFIELD
Chairman, British Airports Authority, 1965—71

Published by
THE INSTITUTE OF ECONOMIC AFFAIRS
1974

First published May 1974
by
THE INSTITUTE OF ECONOMIC AFFAIRS

Printed in Great Britain by
TONBRIDGE PRINTERS LTD, TONBRIDGE, KENT
Set in Intertype Plantin

Preface

IEA OCCASIONAL PAPERS are designed to present material in lectures or papers considered worthy of a larger audience than that to which they were originally addressed. Occasional Paper 40 comprises revised and updated essays based on addresses at a seminar on Maplin chaired by Sir Peter Masefield. The contributors, apart from Sir Peter (as an engineer and a practitioner and analyst of the aircraft, air transport and airport industries), were three economists and an engineer. The Institute was fortunate in persuading Sir Peter to preside over the proceedings. He not only acted as Chairman but also added his judgement and opinion to those of the other contributors.

Professor J. B. Heath begins by indicating the main issues raised by the Maplin project. Professor G. H. Peters reviews the development of cost-benefit analysis on which the report of the Roskill Commission on the third London airport rested its inquiries and recommendations. Professor J. E. Ffowcs Williams reviews the noise aspect which has caused economists and government much thought but on which the natural scientist could shed unique light. Mr Christopher Foster reviews the alternatives to Maplin. And Sir Peter adds his personal interpretation of the essentials.

Professor Heath emphasises that Maplin is not a unique project but one of a series with four characteristics: a long delay between decision and execution, considerable uncertainty, large scale, and government domination. Similar considerations applied to nuclear energy, telephone exchange equipment, Concorde. Such public enterprises invariably disappointed the hopes of politicians, and he thinks it time to ask why. He suggests that it may be the method by which the decisions are made which is at fault. Technical and civil service advice comes to government through a single filter, and government has tended to commit

[5]

itself single-mindedly to what was thought the best solution without going through a process of trial and error:

> 'We went straight for the computerised telephone exchange, straight for supersonic air transport (missing out trans-sonic), more or less straight to production-scale nuclear plants.'

He thinks that more important than the final Maplin outcome are the lessons which should be learnt from it: it is the machinery of government itself that is at fault in failing to develop a system of multiple sources of advice tested by alternative, competitive techniques.

In his essay Professor Peters reviews the strengths and weaknesses of cost-benefit analysis, cost-effectiveness and allied techniques in assessing the social (external) as well as the private (internal) costs and benefits of large projects such as Maplin. He says that the Roskill Commission seemed to have been too easily convinced of the 'need' for a third London airport. In any event, cost-effectiveness techniques did not and could not have demonstrated the superiority of Maplin over Cublington or other sites since it was concerned only with the costs of alternatives and not with their benefits. He joins issue with Professor Sir Colin Buchanan, who argued that the Roskill Commission, in its recommendation of a site, were concerned only with minimum cost and excluded other considerations.

Professor Peters says no estimates were made of the environmental value of Cublington or of Maplin. But no such evaluations could have been made. He maintains the Commission did not assume that costs were the only consideration. Their view was that the site with the lowest cost, Cublington, did not have other defects that put it out of court, and that Maplin did not have other advantages large enough to make its higher cost unimportant. The view of the then Conservative Government – that the difference in cost could be 'traded off' against the environmental advantage of Maplin – embraced value-judgements which Professor Peters maintains make the debate futile.

The interest for economists and others in Professor Ffowcs Williams's contribution is its clear explanation of the impact and cost of noise, the devices to silence it, and the implications for Maplin. On these grounds he, too, is opposed.

Mr Foster's analysis widens the discussion to the aspect emphasised by economists, namely the 'opportunity costs', i.e. the

[6]

alternative uses of scarce resources that would be sacrificed if Maplin were built. He goes on to ask whether the alternatives – in aviation, shipping, land planning and the environment – could secure at least the same benefits as Maplin, but at much lower cost. His conclusion is that on every count the alternatives are superior. Not least, he draws attention to the wider lessons on the methods by which the Conservative Government's commitment to Maplin was reached. He concludes that there has been a political failure to devise the machinery required to avoid a massive waste of public money. He argues that the Treasury failed in its characteristic task of checking large-scale public expenditure, the Cabinet failed in approving the project without sufficient argument or evidence, and both Houses of Parliament failed to scrutinise the project with care. Moreover, if they failed in Maplin, he asks whether they can be relied upon to stop other projects, possibly smaller in scope but equally wasteful in resources. 'If Maplin is built, one consequence should be an overhaul of our traditional and constitutional safeguards against the waste of public funds.'

The new Labour Government has indicated its doubts about going ahead with Maplin. The arguments in this *Occasional Paper* by five observers with varying expertise and philosophic outlook, suggest the case against it is unanswerable, or at least has not been convincingly answered by any government, politician, civil servant, or engineer. But whether it is built or not, the most important conclusion may be the lesson that should be learnt about the machinery of government that can allow such vast projects to be mounted on inadequate grounds. It may be that the market would exclude some projects with a large potential excess of benefits over costs, or that they would be launched on a scale smaller than the optimum. The opposite danger, indicated in this *Paper*, is that government-initiated projects may be launched on too large a scale, technically impressive but economically profligate in alternatives sacrificed, without ensuring adequate attention to the long-term 'public interest'.

In his cogent summing up, Sir Peter Masefield adds the weight of his authority as former Chairman of the British Airports Authority to crystallise the doubts and reservations of the three economists and the engineer. He reviews all the major aspects and concludes with proposals for adapting and expanding Heathrow and Stansted to take the expected increase in traffic. Not least, he draws the general lesson for government decision-making by warning against policies which exclude alternatives that argument and circumstance may make preferable.

The Institute's constitution requires it to dissociate itself from the analyses and conclusions of its authors, but it thanks Sir Peter Masefield and the contributors for assembling a collection of essays of interest to students and teachers of economics and to laymen as a case study in large-scale decision-making in government, its problems and defects, and the urgency of reform.

March 1974 EDITOR

The Authors

JOHN HEATH was educated at St Andrews University and Cambridge. In 1956 he was appointed assistant lecturer and then lecturer in economics at Manchester University. Director of Economic Services Division at the Board of Trade, 1964 to 1970. Professor of Economics at the London School of Business Studies, 1970. He is an Economic Adviser to the Civil Aviation Authority and a member of the Mechanical Engineering EDC.

Author of *Not Enough Competition?* (Hobart Paper 11), Institute of Economic Affairs, 1961 (2nd edn., 1963), articles on productivity, mergers, monopolies and restrictive practices in the learned journals.

GEORGE PETERS was educated at University College, Aberystwyth, and Cambridge. Lecturer in Agricultural Economics at the University of Oxford Agricultural Economics Research Institute, 1959 to 1967. Lecturer in Economics at University of Liverpool, 1967–1969; Senior Lecturer, 1969 to 1970; Brunner Professor of Economic Science, 1970. He is a member of the Royal Statistical Society, Royal Economic Society and the Agricultural Economics Society.

His publications include *Cost-Benefit Analysis and Public Expenditure,* Institute of Economic Affairs, 1966 (2nd edn. 1968, 3rd edn. 1973); *Private and Public Finance,* Fontana/Collins, 1971.

J. E. FFOWCS-WILLIAMS, while an engineering apprentice with Rolls-Royce from 1950 to 1955 won the Spitfire Mitchell Memorial Scholarship to the University of Southampton from 1955 to 1962. Senior Research Fellow at the Aerodynamics Division of the National Physical Laboratory, 1960 to 1962. Senior Scientist of Bolt, Beranek & Newman Inc., Cambridge, Massachusetts, 1962 to 1964. Reader in Applied Mathematics at Imperial College of Science and Technology, 1964 to 1969. Rolls-Royce Professor of Theoretical Acoustics at Imperial College, 1969 to 1972. Rank Professor of Engineering (Acoustics), University of Cambridge, since 1972. Fellow of the Institute of Mathematics and its Applications; Cambridge Philosophical

Society; Acoustical Society of America; Royal Aeronautical Society; Institute of Physics. Chairman of the Aeronautical Research Council Noise Research Committee. He has written on aerodynamic noise in several learned journals.

CHRISTOPHER FOSTER was educated at King's College, Cambridge. Research Fellow at the University of Manchester, 1957 to 1959. Fellow of Jesus College, Oxford, 1959 to 1966. Senior Economic Adviser on Regional Problems to the Department of Economic Affairs (DEA), 1965. Director-General of Economic Planning, Ministry of Transport, 1966 to 1969. Visiting Professor, Massachusetts Institute of Technology, 1969 to 1970. Head of the Centre for Urban Economics at the London School of Economics since 1970.

His published work includes *The Transport Problem*, Blackie, 1963; *Politics, Finance and the Role of Economics*, Allen and Unwin, 1972; *Urban Transport Policy*, World Bank, 1971; *Public Enterprise*, Fabian Research Series No. 300, 1972. He has written on transport, cost-benefit analysis, urban problems, nationalised industries and public finance in most of the learned journals.

SIR PETER MASEFIELD was born in 1914 and educated at Westminster School and Jesus College, Cambridge; trained as an engineer (MA Cantab., CEng, FRAeS, FCIT); on the design staff of Fairey Aviation, 1935–37; he then joined the journal, *The Aeroplane*, and became technical editor, 1939–43, and air correspondent of the *Sunday Times*, 1940–43. War correspondent, advisor to Government on civil aviation and first British Civil Air Attaché to the British Embassy in Washington. After a period as director-general of long-term planning at the Ministry of Civil Aviation he became Chief Executive of BEA, 1949–55; Managing Director, Bristol Aircraft Ltd., 1956–60, and Beagle Aircraft, 1960–67 (then Chairman); Chairman, British Airports Authority, 1965–71. He is Chairman of Project Management Ltd. and a member of the Board of the LTE.

Sir Peter's public career includes membership of the Cairns Committee on Aircraft Accident Investigation, 1960; President of the Royal Aeronautical Society, 1959–60; Chairman, Royal Aero Club of the United Kingdom, 1968–74. Author of numerous articles on aeronautical and transport subjects in the technical press.

Introduction
RALPH HARRIS

THE IEA will be known to many of you as the home of lost markets. Its authors, including two of the present contributors, have characteristically directed attention to the legal and institutional environment of markets and pricing which may (avoidably) distort the application of scarce resources. But as evidence of its well-known impartiality, IEA authors have – in addition to analysing 'market failure' – not entirely overlooked what I might call 'government failure' which has led to large and avoidable waste in atomic energy,[1] high technology,[2] nationalised industries and other forgotten or less visible corners of 'public' (government) policy.

There will be general agreement, among economists at least, that the problem to which long ago Berle and Means drew our attention of the divorce between ownership and control in joint stock companies has its counterpart writ large in the 'public' sector. Where long-term investment decisions are taken by politicians for the time being in command of the governmental apparatus, there is a divorce between control and ultimate financial responsibility.

Thus it is an axiom of economists not in the pay of private interests that we cannot take for granted that directors of public companies will always act in the long-term interest of their shareholders or, indeed, of anyone else. Hence the need for the checks and balances provided by modern company law, by vigorous competition, and by an alert financial press. In the same spirit we should be sceptical whether Ministers can be assumed to weigh all the relevant factors in coming to large decisions about the application of national resources underwritten compulsorily by the taxpayers.

[1] Duncan Burn, *The Political Economy of Nuclear Energy*, Research Monograph 9, IEA, 1967.

[2] John Jewkes, *Government and High Technology*, Third Wincott Memorial Lecture, Occasional Paper 37, IEA, 1972.

Let me offer you some warning signals of advanced rake's progress. The temptation for extravagant window-dressing will always be strong where a political decision has strong appeal to expediency, can be represented as 'visionary', coincides with pressure from a vocal lobby, and involves the immediate commitment of large investments for distant objectives the value of which cannot be finally assessed until many years and an election or two later. It is here that *independent* scholars and commentators have a special responsibility to apply the best tests they can devise to the claims and calculations of the temporary incumbents of government.

Many economic commentators, particularly in journalism and television, repeatedly rehearse the imperfections of private enterprise but rarely those of the legal framework within which it operates. Much less attention has been focused in the post-war years on the larger failings of 'public' enterprise which appear far harder to eradicate in a society conferring powers on politicians and civil servants less easily disciplined by legal, financial or institutional sanctions.[1] The commitment of Mr Heath's Government to the Maplin project was chosen for examination as a case study in public policy formation which might teach lessons of much wider application in the use of scarce national resources.

[1]An attempt to devise a market-orientated system of rewards and penalties for bureaucrats has been made by Professor William A. Niskanen in *Bureaucracy: Servant or Master?*, Hobart Paperback No. 5, IEA, 1973.

I. The Central Issues
J. B. HEATH[1]

Professor of Economics,
London School of Business Studies

THE PURPOSE of this IEA *Paper* is to examine some of the economic issues that would appear to be important in the Maplin
controversy that have so far received little public discussion, and
to put them in the context of the wider set of issues related to
Maplin. My role is to set the stage and to ask some pertinent
questions.

I would like to start from a point that Ralph Harris made
earlier, when he reminded us that Maplin is one of a series of
large projects, involving similar types of characteristics. They
all require a long delay between the decision and its implementa-
tion, they involve high degrees of uncertainty, either technological or marketing, or both, they are all large-scale, they are
all in the government domain. They include decisions relating
to nuclear energy, telephone exchange equipment, Concorde,
North Sea oil and gas, to mention but a few.

Experience – and reasons
Of the earlier projects on which a judgement can now be
made, one outstanding feature is that many have turned out
to be wrong in at least one important respect. I think
it is worth pausing to reflect on some possible reasons why they
went bad, and whether any lessons can yet be drawn. In this
way some light may be cast on the underlying problems that
relate to Maplin.

The subject is large and deserves careful study. I believe the
issue is *how* such decisions are made, how and at what level
conflicting views are resolved, what system the Minister (or
generally, because of the importance of the issues we are con-

---

[1] May I first issue a disclaimer on behalf of myself and one or two
colleagues also here from the Civil Aviation Authority; we are of course
speaking in our personal capacities and not as representatives of the
Authority.

sidering, the Cabinet) uses to generate advice, and, more fundamentally, whether such decisions should be made at the political level at all.

In his very interesting study, *The Political Economy of Nuclear Energy*,[1] Duncan Burn has shown the way. He put the view that a competitive situation has to be created, competitive within government but preferably some kind of market-place competition outside government. There must be a genuine forum in which competition between alternative ways of proceeding with that project can be acted through. He pointed out that in the United States the federal Government supported the nuclear power programme with roughly the same volume of resources as the British Government, but that they went about it very differently. There was no single stream of technical advice (as in this country through the Atomic Energy Authority), no single stream of civil service advice (here through the administrative class civil servants). Decisions were dispersed. Moreover, in the United States they did not close their options at any early stage on the final decision, but proceeded by stages, hedging their bets by putting substantial resources into a number of different possible lines of development, until the right one became clear. There has been a marked tendency in this country to go straight for what was thought at the time to be the ultimate solution, without going through the intermediate stages. We went straight for the computerised telephone exchange, straight for supersonic air transport (missing out trans-sonic), more or less straight to production-scale nuclear plants. All of these turned out to be disastrously wrong. Why did we do it? We have never lacked the experts. I believe that it is our traditional system of decision-making that has let us down in these cases, and that has also landed us with the present controversy over Maplin. What I am saying is that I believe we have in this country a severe management problem in the business of government. That is the real issue.

Part of this management problem is to ensure that the correct questions are asked. It is noticeable, as Sir Peter Masefield has said, that the focus of current discussion is quite different from the focus of concentration of the Roskill Commission. Then it was alternative sites, now it is whether or not we need the

[1]Research Monograph 9, IEA, 1967.

airport at all. I believe that neither is correct. Should we not think much more about *alternative strategies for managing London and regional airport capacity* under conditions of uncertainty about future demand? It is difficult for a government wishing to make a single firm decision to think along these lines; but I believe that this is the best way to express the problem so long as what should ultimately be done remains unknown.

Is cost-benefit analysis relevant?

The Roskill Commission used fundamentally a cost-benefit approach. With hindsight, what lessons can be drawn from this experience? What is the relevance now, in the present circumstances of the Maplin controversy, of cost-benefit analysis? How should we analyse the view now being expressed that Maplin is the Rotterdam of England – that it will be better than Rotterdam because it will have a major airport as well as a seaport, a modern purpose-built network of surface communications and so on? Now that we are in the EEC, let us face our new partners with a living demonstration of how we can face the future with confidence, with skill and imagination. It is this vision – it is said – that really matters.

Is this capable of rational analysis by cost-benefit or some other technique? Must not even visions of this kind make economic sense in the long run? These are among the issues that Professor George Peters discusses in his paper on cost-benefit analysis.

Maplin and regionalism

One topic which seems to me of importance, and which has not entered the current controversy, is the relationship between the Maplin development and regional development. Roskill paid lip-service to it. Likewise the South-East Study team did not fully take account of the possibility of a Maplin airport and seaport and all that they would imply. Two years have gone by since then, with a lot more understanding about the *process* of regional development, its dynamics and the systems of control. Where do we now stand with all of this in relation to Maplin? Does it remain the important issue that Professor Buchanan sought to make it? I still do not understand the mechanics by which that improvement to the East End of London which he emphasised would occur. Might not the East End remain the poor area of Maplin New Town?

And perhaps we should consider Maplin also in the context of the possible development of a new route that by-passes London from the South coast. I am thinking of the Channel Tunnel, taking in Maplin on the way before joining with the main routes to the North. Is this a viable regional context in which to see Maplin?

Noise

Much of the recent debate has been conducted by economists and operational research people, and there has been very little public discussion by technologists, by the engineers and the people who understand the basis of the technological forecasts for aircraft noise. They are most familiar with the likely costs of technological change, with the time-scale that may be involved, and consequently with the wider question whether the country may be better off putting resources into making aircraft quieter than in developing Maplin. Are these really alternatives, or are they complementary in terms of development? Professor Ffowcs Williams, Rank Professor of Engineering (Acoustics) at the University of Cambridge, tackles these questions.

'Political' aspect

Then there is the question of the management of Maplin in its political and its managerial context. What would *we* now do if we were rational beings in positions of authority, taking account both of the political realities of the situation and of the management problems under conditions of uncertainty. In Essay No. IV, Mr Christopher Foster examines some possibilities. What, for example, does one say to those who claim that the environmentalists are becoming so powerful in this country (and elsewhere) that if Maplin does not go ahead now we shall never get it at all? Is it a now-or-never situation? If so, what strategy does it imply for the management of capacity at London's airports? No one can say positively that we shall never need to have a new airport in the London area – we simply do not know.

And finally there is the point managers often make, that even if the decision is not obviously right, can it not be engineered to come right? The test of good management, some would say, is to make a success of a poor decision (others would argue that it is much safer in the long run to improve the quality of the decision). What has to be done to make Maplin a success? Is it feasible? Is it cost-effective?

These are some of the issues we discuss in this IEA *Paper*.

II. Cost-Benefit Analysis and the Third London Airport

G. H. PETERS

Brunner Professor of Economic Science, University of Liverpool

THE MAIN objective of this paper will be to ask whether the cost-benefit analysis in the Roskill Report is of much help in considering the controversy now developing around the Maplin project. A brief general resumé of the methods employed in cost-benefit studies will be followed by a description and appraisal of the manner in which the Roskill team approached their task. The main content of the paper is not an exhaustive attempt to rake through the details of the Report[1] but a rough sketch map guide to the analysis, which will focus primarily on the general method of approach, allied to a small amount of analysis of some of the trickier issues the research team had to face.

COST-BENEFIT ANALYSIS[2]

It is not uncommon to see the term 'cost-benefit analysis' prefaced by the word 'social'. Similarly we often hear references to 'cost-effectiveness' techniques. Anyone who reads economic literature soon senses that such jargon can easily become a source of confusion unless its meaning is understood. To come to grips with the subject it is easiest to begin by considering the general process of economic appraisal: what steps must one go through before one can regard investment as economically worthwhile?

The usual method for testing the 'soundness' of proposed activities involves a calculation of the value of resources to be employed in them (the costs) which are compared with the value

---

[1]The final form of the cost-benefit analysis is to be found in Commission on the Third London Airport (CTLA), *Report*, HMSO, London, 1971, especially Ch. 12 and Appendix 20, which presents modifications to the research team's assessment in CTLA, *Papers and Proceedings*, Volume VII, HMSO, London, 1970.

[2]A more detailed exposition is in G. H. Peters, *Cost-Benefit Analysis and Public Expenditure*, Eaton Paper 8, IEA, 3rd edn., 1973.

of the goods or services to be produced (the benefits). In appraising commercial investments the normal practice is to subtract all variable or running costs from sales receipts, leaving a residual expressed as an annual rate of return on the capital employed. If the anticipated returns compare favourably with the prospective returns from alternative uses, the proposed project may be regarded as 'sound' from the point of view of a private business. Of course the rate of return must also exceed the cost of obtaining capital as expressed through the rate of interest.

In a competitive market economy – and indeed this is its object – the value of benefits yielded by an activity is reflected through the price mechanism in the amounts which ultimate consumers are prepared to pay for goods and services. Similarly the costs are reflected through markets for the factors of production – labour, capital, land, entrepreneurial talents. In the last analysis, of course, these costs must be related to consumers' valuations of the goods which would have become available if resources had been used in other ways. They are 'opportunity costs,' or the measure of the value of alternative lines of activity. If the returns on capital in one use, after allowing for the degree of risk associated with it, are higher than those in other uses, the forces of competition will tend to bring about transfers of resources from areas of low to areas of higher return unless this movement is frustrated by lack of information or other influences. That returns may be different is of course a reflection of consumers' preferences, improvements in technique and the development of knowledge; and re-allocation consequent upon changes in any of them represents a useful social function in best allocating resources between competing uses.

Resource allocation: importance of rates of return
Though this picture of a market economy is an idealised one it serves to emphasise the critical importance of rates of return as a dominant variable in the process of resource allocation. For our purposes (and this is a simplification adopted purely because space is short), we can say that interest in cost-benefit analysis has arisen primarily for two reasons:

a) A large part of economic activity is now associated with the public provision of goods and services (defence, roads, higher education, health services, environmental services, etc.) whose *costs* are known. However, so far as the beneficiaries are concerned such services are provided on a non-market basis – they are 'free.' We do not indicate, *in the market,* our demands for additional roads, or universities, or hospitals. Decisions concerning the scale of the supply are left, basically, to the political process – they rest with ministers and public officials, and ultimately, in a rather crude way, with the ballot box. However what has happened, quite simply, is that a search has been going on for tools for the economic appraisal of public supply which will serve to sharpen the process of decision-making. It is here that cost-benefit analysis has made its appearance. In short attempts are made to ask whether benefits, measured in some way, will exceed the known costs of provision.

b) Our second reason is associated with the distinction between private and social costs and benefits made famous at the beginning of the century by the late Professor A. C. Pigou. In the course of his treatise on welfare economics Pigou pointed out that there may be circumstances in which market forces fail to encompass all costs and/or all benefits. In his own words:

'The essence of the matter is that one person A, in the course of rendering some service for which payment is made, to a second person B, incidentally also renders services or disservices to other persons, of such sort that payment cannot be extracted from the benefited parties or compensation enforced on behalf of the injured parties.'[3]

In this context social costs may be defined as the sum total of costs that result from an economic action. Private costs are those which affect the decisions of its performers. For example, in production undertaken for a market, what are the private costs with which the entrepreneur is concerned? First, he must pay labour at least as much as it would be worth in other uses; he must compete for materials, land and capital; he must earn his rewards. All of these also represent 'opportunity costs' to society at large. They are social costs reflected through the market. Over and above them, however, may be additional 'ex-

[3] A. C. Pigou, *The Economics of Welfare,* 4th edn., Macmillan, 1950, p. 183.

ternal' costs not impinging on the entrepreneur; the examples of smoke and noise nuisance are well known.

Externalities and rates of return
Similar effects may occur on the other side of the equation. Benefits are reflected in the amounts paid by consumers for goods produced; but, in addition, favourable 'externalities' might also accrue to society. An example is a dam which, in addition to generating electricity for sale in the market, provides flood protection benefits for which no payment is made. If there are external costs, the private rate of return on capital, which is what interests the entrepreneur, over-states the social returns; while, conversely, it may under-estimate the social return if there are external benefits.

In the words of Professor Alan Prest and Mr Ralph Turvey, who have written one of the most authoritative surveys of cost-benefit methodology:

'Cost-benefit analysis is a practical way of assessing the desirability of projects, where it is important to take a long view (in the sense of looking at repercussions in the further, as well as the nearer, future) and a wide view (in the sense of allowing for side effects of many kinds on many persons, industries, regions, etc.) i.e. it implies the enumeration and evaluation of all the relevant costs and benefits.'[4]

What all this means, of course, is that a project should be undertaken only if its benefits (suitably discounted) exceed its costs. A project, in this sense, could involve governmental provision of a community service (examples appear under [a] above) or a private investment deemed by public officials to have such wide-ranging external effects that a fuller social appraisal of its worth should be undertaken (examples include water resource development projects, discussed below). The pervading snag, and indeed the major challenge facing the cost-benefit analyst who wishes to engage in a wide-ranging *social* evaluation, is that market-based indications of costs and benefits *may be incomplete*. Three examples illustrate the importance of this point:

[4]A. R. Prest and R. Turvey, 'Cost-Benefit Analysis: A Survey', *Economic Journal*, December 1965, reprinted in R. Layard (ed.), *Cost-Benefit Analysis*, Penguin Modern Economics Readings, Penguin Books, 1972.

(1) In appraising road investments there is no market indicator of *benefits*. The appropriate values accruing from roads have been estimated largely on the basis of *time-* and *cost-*savings, with the former assuming paramount importance. This type of work was pioneered in the Road Research Laboratory/University of Birmingham study of the MI and is now done, as a matter of routine, by the Department of the Environment in the analysis of major road changes. The main problem is time valuation, which will be discussed when we turn to the Roskill analysis. Externalities are taken into account if the construction of a new route, because of a decrease in congestion, leads to time- and cost-savings on existing roads.

(2) American water resource development studies provide examples of the first area in which cost-benefit analysis was applied and developed. The construction of a dam, though its primary aim is the generation of electricity for sale, may lead to external benefits in flood protection (appraised by studies of the incidence and extent of flood damage) or additional irrigation potential (appraised by calculations of the contribution extra water might make to agricultural value added). These cases provide an excellent illustration of divergence between private rates of return based solely on the value of additional electricity generation, and (often higher) social rates of return with externalities included.

(3) Expenditure on higher education has been appraised by setting off the additional earnings of those who have reached the higher rungs of the education ladder against additional education costs. This is a very difficult calculation since incremental earnings may be ascribed not only to education but also, presumably, to ability. A recent British study[5] placed the rate of return on higher education to first degree level at 9.2 per cent (just below the trial rate of discount used in nationalised industry investment appraisal), and the incremental return to higher degrees at zero. It is a worrying time for academics who normally reply that the

[5]V. Morris and A. Ziderman, 'The Economic Return on Investment in Higher Education in England and Wales', *Economic Trends*, HMSO, May 1971.

calculations emphasise only *economic* returns ('investment') and leave out the 'consumption' aspects of higher education!

Other examples could be cited, but all that really needs to be said is that a wide-ranging survey of a project's viability involves utilising market-based monetary valuations of costs and benefits where one can, and *imputing* values where one cannot, in order to arrive at a *total* assessment of costs and benefits. The obstacles which face the cost-benefit analyst in attaining his goal of a full appraisal can be enormous, particularly insofar as they relate to the imputed items. Cost-benefit analysis gets its worst press when there is considerable difficuty in imputation – how can values be attached to noise or pollution disbenefits, to health as such, to the value of life, to recreational amenity, or to the wider benefits of education? The analysis can easily run into quicksand and invite the retort of Professor Peter Self, specifically on the Roskill study, that cost-benefit analysis is nothing more than 'nonsense-on-stilts'.[6]

The 'cost-effectiveness' approach

In some circumstances a partial escape may be found in the so-called 'cost-effectiveness' approach. If a project is designed to serve a particular purpose, or if its results can be measured according to some non-monetary scale, choice of method, or choice of scale may be aided by careful costing of each alternative. In defence studies, for example, it is impossible to conceive of a monetary value being placed on 'being defended' on the basis of which one might choose the optimum scale of defence – but there is obvious sense in studying, on a cost-effectiveness basis, the potency of weapon systems in relation to costs; the cost of reducing risks to shipping; or the costs of alternative defensive arrangements. The cost-effectiveness approach (often dressed up in the form of a 'goals achievement matrix' or as a 'planning balance-sheet') is also common in town re-development studies and in regional planning. But these methods are 'lower level' that the full-blooded cost-benefit study which sets all costs against all benefits, each expressed in monetary terms, thus providing a clear guide (assuming the difficulties of quantification have been resolved) on whether to pro-

[6]P. Self, ' "Nonsense-on-Stilts": Cost-Benefit Analysis and the Roskill Commission', *Political Quarterly*, 1970.

ceed with a project. The cost-effectiveness method can only take a 'need' as given and seek for the cheapest mode of provision.

THE ROSKILL COST-BENEFIT ANALYSIS

Basically the major part of the Roskill study appears to have been founded on the *assumption* that the need for a third airport was firmly established. Though this is a rather strong statement, for reasons which will be mentioned presently, it is only against such a background that one can fully appreciate the fundamental basis of the work done. The crux of the matter is that, given such a starting point, the problem resolved itself into the detailed costing of airport provision at each potential site and the choice of the cheapest alternative.[7] Indeed the process which formed the bulk of the research team's work, and on which the press concentrated at the time of publication, was basically a cost-effectiveness study. For this reason the results summarised in the Table are set out in terms of costs and do not directly mention benefits. The latter appear only in a very obscure way (below, p. 25).

THE THIRD LONDON AIRPORT—COST-BENEFIT ANALYSIS
(£ million discounted to 1982)

	Cublington		Foulness		Nuthampstead		Thurleigh	
Airport construction*	303		335		300		283	
Airport services	127	(113)	104	(91)	121	(108)	111	(98)
Agriculture	8		11		16		10	
Airspace movement costs	1,899	(1,685)	1,906	(1,690)	1,934	(1,716)	1,929	(1,711)
User costs	2,903	(1,763)	3,124	(1,944)	2,949	(1,803)	2,942	(1,785)
Road and rail capital	39		67		52		41	
Defence	73		44		49		105	
Noise	23		21		72		16	
Other costs†	58		18		77		84	
Total costs	5,433	(4,065)	5,630	(4,221)	5,570	(4,193)	5,521	(4,133)
Aggregate of inter-site differences	0		197	(156)	137	(128)	88	(68)

Source: Roskill Commission *Report*, Appendix 20; Table 12.1 for the aggregate of inter-site differences, and other detailed tables for the estimates under each head. Bracketed figures are based on 'low' time values.

*Including Luton extensions. For Foulness these would cost £20 million compared with £2.5 million in other cases.

†Meteorology, air safety, scientific establishments, private airfields, on-site residential conditions, public buildings, commerce and industry, recreation.

[7]Though the main work related only to four potential short-listed sites these had, in turn, been selected from an initial list of 78 possible locations.

The Table reveals a number of cost items for which valuation problems raised no large issues of principle. These include airport construction costs (note that the resource costs absorbed by Foulness are shown to be £32 million higher than those estimated for Cublington, £52 million more than the Thurleigh figure), costs of provision of airport services (water, sewage, electricity, etc.), defence costs (associated mainly with moving various military establishments), agricultural land values, and the capital necessary to provide road and rail links. The item 'other costs' covers a heterogeneous bunch of factors (including such minutiae as the much debated value of Stewkley Church) which we will not discuss in detail. We are left with airspace movement costs, user costs, and noise.

Cost calculations – a critique

The first two were critically affected by alternative assumptions about the value of time (the bracketed figures relating to low time-values) and by the accuracy of the forecasts of airport use. Airspace movement costs vary partly because the alternative sites were expected to attract different levels of utilisation, but also because flying time between the airport and the start of the major air lanes at the edges of the London air traffic control sector would differ depending upon airport location (aircraft using the North Atlantic route, for example, would travel further to reach Foulness than Cublington). The costs measured therefore included both aircraft operation and travellers' time. Similarly, user costs included rail fares or road transport costs plus time valuations, the number of passengers affected again varying with airport location. Here, however, there is a snag. The traffic forecasts indicated that by the year 2000 usage of Foulness would be some 7 per cent lower than at Cublington, and also less than for the other two sites; in short there is a relationship between accessibility and traffic flows. Since cost differences are the key to the final recommendation it would be wrong to ignore this link – implicitly one would tilt the balance in favour of the least accessible site! A way therefore had to be found for crediting all sites other than Foulness with a value reflecting their more convenient situation.

The calculations were complex since they involved the manipulation of a 'gravity model' for forecasting traffic flows, which would indicate the extra trips generated by the choice of any of the inland sites. Following the example of other transport studies, the value to be placed on such 'generated traffic' was recorded at one-half of the time- and cost-savings advantage of the inland site compared with Foulness. Hence the figures shown for Cublington, Nuthampstead and Thurleigh are the basic user costs *minus* the imputed advantages accruing to them because of their locational superiority for airport users.

Since airport user costs and airspace movement costs assume such large importance in the whole exercise their valuation is of vital significance. And since cost differences arise as residual differences between very large totals, they can be critically affected by changes in the underlying aggregates. Furthermore, since both items include time valuations, it was important that these values should be carefully examined. The original research study split travellers into 'business' and 'leisure' categories, valuing time for the former at the average hourly cost of employment (£2.32). Leisure passengers' time-values were put at 23 pence and 5 pence per hour for adults and children respectively. These figures (for 1968) were estimated to grow by approximately 3 per cent per annum to reach hourly values of £3.60 for businessmen and 41 pence and 14 pence for adults and children.[8] Realising that time values are open to question, the Commission decided to use 'high' and 'low' figures in their final report. For businessmen these were £2.58 and £1.46 per hour, while for leisure time the values were 50 per cent above and below those employed in the research study.

Putting a value on noise

In considering valuation problems we must turn, finally, to noise. For comparative purposes it is interesting to note that some 700,000 households are within the noise 'shadow' of

[8]Leisure time here is valued on Department of the Environment standards which now regard time as worth 25 per cent of the hourly wage-earnings of travellers – the 3 per cent factor accounts for growth in living standards. No real justification is provided for applying these values to non-working members of the travelling public, and the allowance for children remained virtually unexplained.

Heathrow.[9] Estimates of those likely to be similarly afflicted by the third airport were 95,000 for Nuthampstead, and 20,000–30,000 for the alternative sites.

The valuation procedure was particularly complex. We are considering one of those extremely difficult areas of cost-benefit methodology in which imputation is necessary. Put briefly, householders affected by a build-up of noise can react either by suffering a worsening of their living conditions, or by moving. In the latter event their loss would consist of two elements, property depreciation (including removal costs) and the loss of 'householders' surplus'. The former was estimated by a survey of the property market in the Gatwick airport area which showed that there is a relationship between noise intensity and house prices.[10]

Put simply, the concept of 'householders' surplus' refers to the amount of money over and above the market price of property which owners would require to induce them to make a willing sale: it reflects such factors as personal ties to a house, locality or circle of friends. From a survey in areas unlikely to be affected by noise the average value of householders' surplus was placed at 39 per cent above market values, though attempts were made to recognise that the precise figure can vary between householders. There are two obvious problems at this stage: forecasting the number of households likely to move, whose 'loss' could be estimated by the method just described, and ascribing a noise nuisance value to non-movers. Here previous evidence, based on psycho-sociological survey material, was used to obtain a frequency distribution, for each NNI (noise and nuisance index) value, showing the proportion of persons within the population who expressed varying degrees of annoyance with aircraft disturbance (some, apparently, are 'imperturbable)'. The annoyance scores taken as an index were then translated into monetary values by assuming that the median score could

[9]Noise levels are now measured by a 'noise and nuisance index' (NNI) which is a weighted average of noise intensity and frequency. Those 'affected' are taken as members of households within the 35 NNI contour – in the event of an airport being built many more people would be disturbed to a lesser degree.

[10]Percentage rates of depreciation rose to 29 per cent for the most expensive property in the noisiest areas, and to about a third of this figure for the cheapest homes.

be equated with the average property depreciation in the Gatwick area at the appropriate NNI level. This exercise may appear completely outlandish – until it is remembered that 'depreciated' property is sold on the market, and the 'discount' obtained is presumably related to the purchasers' subjective valuation of the disamenity of noise.[11] Given this type of information, movement was forecast by estimating the number of households for whom noise nuisance values were likely to be *larger than* the sum of depreciation and householders' surplus, the latter two items being taken as their total noise loss. The non-movers were then allotted an imputed nuisance cost depending on the translation of the annoyance level scores into money values (as described above), and the supposed underlying frequency distribution.

THE ROSKILL COMMISSION – APPRAISAL

In appraising the work of the Roskill Commission one point can be disposed of immediately. There is apparently a widespread impression (fostered partly by Professor Colin Buchanan's 'Note of Dissent') that the Commission were prepared to recommend the choice of Cublington as the lowest-cost site regardless of all other considerations. Certainly no estimates were made of the environmental worth of the Cublington site, or of the ecological and recreational value of Maplin Sands. Nor did the Commission place a value on the possibility of a Foulness development triggering off 'a regenerative process reaching right back into the heart of London where the East End butts against the City'.[12] There is no way in which such valuations could be made. But a reading of Chapter 6, which deals with land-use planning, should be enough to convince anyone that the Com-

---

[11]The *Report, op. cit.,* Appendix 22, contains a long account of other possible assumptions. For example, purchasers of 'noisy' property could well be persons whose 'noise annoyance' score is below the median (i.e. the more 'imperturbable'). Use of the 'lower quartile' as the equating point would raise noise costs by about 50 per cent.

[12]'Note of Dissent', *Report,* p. 158. Professor Buchanan's view was that the eastern side of London is an economically and socially disadvantaged area, particularly in comparison with the west, and that a regenerative effect could arise if a major new source of employment became available. The locational advantages of the area would presumably also be strengthened to some degree.

mission were alive to the possibility that costs alone, as identified in the analysis, should be viewed as but one piece of relevant evidence. Their argument simply was that the lowest-cost site did not have other disadvantages associated with it which would make it unacceptable, and that the Foulness development would not so foster the achievement of wider planning goals as to make its cost disadvantage unimportant. The 1970–74 Government took a different view – it is a question of 'trading off' a cost disparity against a range of qualitative factors. Since this choice must involve value-judgements, debate can become futile.

It could be argued, however, that the Commission were somewhat over-assertive in emphasising the magnitude of the costed inferiority of the Foulness site, which they placed at £156–£197 million. The estimates were based on an inherently difficult long-period traffic forecast and (as we will see in a moment) some valuations are also open to suspicion. In terms of identified costs, development of Foulness was shown to be some 3.6 or 3.8 per cent more expensive than Cublington – a very narrow margin when all the uncertainties and difficulties are considered.[13]

Valuation controversy

The two costing items which have attracted controversy are travelling time and noise. The first of these is not unexpected. It was in this item that the inferiority of Foulness became particularly marked. The point is familiar enough – can leisure time (often of only small duration for each individual) be valued by reference to earnings? Are housewives' and children's time-savings amenable to sensible treatment? Does a businessman's delay inflict severe opportunity costs on the nation as a whole? The Commission argued that time *is* important and stuck to the basic logic of their approach. What they failed to point out was

[13]Here it is interesting to note that the research team's analysis did not set out costs in the general form shown in the table. We have already mentioned that the *Report* focussed particular attention only on inter-site differences – the totals, it was said (*Report*, p. 118), have no relevance. This is true, but the research team were far more ready to admit of possible error than the Commission seemed to be, and more willing to inquire assiduously into the sensitivity of the results.

that their calculations rested on a flimsy basis.[14] As Dr E. J. Mishan has observed, there is

> 'clearly some margin to be got by playing around with such figures, and this makes any choice on economic grounds alone appear somewhat less satisfactory'.[15]

On noise, there are two aspects of the Commission's procedure which can be questioned. First, the estimation of 'householders' surplus' was obtained (as we have seen) from a sample survey conducted in areas unlikely to be affected by airport noise – indeed people were asked to imagine their reactions to a situation in which their homes were wanted 'to form part of a large development scheme' and that a developer was making an offer to purchase. Though a sum above market price necessary to compensate for the loss of 'householders' surplus' can be derived in this way, the natural reaction of those questioned would very possibly be to assume that they could *move a short distance* away and suffer little or no dislocation of their social and working lives. The resulting figures do not necessarily bear any relation to the amount necessary to compensate people who find that their *whole locality* is invaded by noise from which they cannot escape without *major* disruption.[16]

Question of 'need' for new airport not answered

These are not the most fundamental criticisms, however. The basic point is that a cost-effectiveness study, by its nature, cannot in itself establish a *'need'* for a third airport and cannot show whether the total costs of construction and operation will be smaller than the benefits it will confer. Of course one could not expect that a research team of the expertise assembled to aid the Commission would be so foolish as to ignore the whole question of the 'value to the nation of a third London airport'. However, in Volume VII of the supplementary papers, which

[14]The research team's work showed that the removal of leisure time-savings from the calculation, and the reduction of the value of business time by 25 per cent from £2.32 per hour made Thurleigh the least-cost site. Cublington's advantage over Foulness was reduced to £32 million.

[15]E. J. Mishan, 'What is Wrong with Roskill?', *Journal of Transport Economics and Policy*, 1971, reprinted in Layard, *op. cit.*

[16]This criticism is again due to Mishan, *ibid.*

contains the research team's very detailed assessment and which runs to 510 pages, only one short chapter of five pages was devoted to the issue. Indeed it contains the telling sentences:

> 'It is not enough to state that an investment can be justified purely by the public demand for the services it provides. It must also be demonstrated that the demand is sufficiently strong to outweigh all costs and disbenefits which are incurred, particularly if some of these are not directly met by air traffic revenue.'[17]

In short, what is being said is that an airport, anywhere, can be regarded as economically worthwhile only if it can cover its capital and operating costs *and also* (and this is the crunch) if it is so in demand that it can charge fees sufficient also to cover the disamenities it creates. Now it is true that the chapter quoted does contain a very short calculation showing that commercial viability could be ensured given a rise in landing fees – but it never goes the whole way. Instead, as Mishan has observed, we are treated to a recital of a number of factors (growing popularity of the package tour, aids to business travel, benefits to the aircraft industry and so on) which seem to be put forward to 'convince the public that the benefits are almost self-evident'.[18]

Similarly, in their work on the 'timing of the need' the research team simply attempted to estimate the likely growth of congestion costs at Heathrow and Gatwick (made up of extra operating costs and time losses) and to forecast that point in the future at which these would exceed the imputed interest charges (10 per cent on construction costs) plus operating expenses of a new airport – 1980 being the date chosen. Now the inclusion of such calculations is of course a point in the Commission's favour – their answer could have been 'never'. However it remains true that we simply do not know whether air transport, at any airport anywhere (including Heathrow), is so in demand as to be capable of covering capital and operating

[17]*CTLA*, Vol. VII, *op. cit.*, p. 103.

[18]Mishan, *op. cit.*

costs *and* the value of disamenities created.[19] Until this question is answered against the background of all the accumulating knowledge about new transport developments, we are in no position at all to conclude that a third airport should be built. Certainly a cost-effectiveness study of locational choice, such as that contained in the Roskill Report, cannot provide a firm basis for a major policy decision.

[19]This point, of course, follows from the distinction between private and social costs. Airports provide a commercial service for which fees are charged. However the 'private' rate of return on capital investment may, given the externalities, under-value the 'social' returns. The initial problem, basically, is the fundamental structure of airport pricing. It is also worth noting that the criticisms made of the noise valuations are particularly important in this context.

III. How Much Noise?

J. E. FFOWCS WILLIAMS

Rank Professor of Engineering (Acoustics),
University of Cambridge

I WON'T try and put noise in any format which could be labelled cost-benefit analysis, since I am frankly appalled by the apparent lack of science in that procedure. Everyone who has his wits about him knows that noise is probably the most important issue in determining whether Maplin goes ahead or not, yet it appears in the cost-benefit analysis by the Roskill Commission as I per cent of the total bill which fails miserably to give due importance to this item. It seems to me that cost-benefit analysis is not a rational way of assessing the importance of various elements, but merely a numerate way. It is wrong to think that, because something can be quantified, quantification is necessarily relevant.

Acoustics often provides good examples of such a mistaken reverence for numbers. The 'reverberation time' of a hall is very easily measured, and because of this architects tend to think it significant, and it is very often not.

Town or country?

But noise is important and we all want to eliminate the airport noise problem. But to suggest that it could be eliminated by building an airport at Maplin is as stupid as the notion that the noise of cities would be eliminated if cities were sited in the country. Firstly, the airport would draw its own community, which initially no doubt would have a vested interest and would not complain about noise. For them it will be nice to hear flying overhead the aircraft which are bringing along their bread and butter. But secondary services will then be building up in the community, and of course the second generation will come along which will be less interested in the airport. They will no doubt complain and we will be back to square one. Perhaps the problem will not be as bad as that currently experienced at Heathrow; nonetheless we can expect a substantial volume of complaints from the populations near any large airport. Also if the airport is out in the country, I am sure it will be very difficult indeed to make aircraft so quiet that they will be regarded as inaudible above a quiet background.

I have no doubt at all that, on the time-scale of twenty years, we could make aircraft quiet enough to ensure that they would not be heard above an urban background. I strongly doubt whether we could ever make aircraft inaudible against a country background. It seems to me to be a rather important point. If we restrict the airport noise to areas where there is already a hubbub, we are quite likely to be able to cure the problem more easily than if we move the airport away to a virgin area. At the moment we can retire there to peace and quiet if we want to, but the airport will destroy that amenity.

Assumptions

I will start my discussion on further possibilities and the costs of noise control by stating my ground rules. The first is that air transportation is 'good' for mankind. Secondly, the aircraft building industry is also 'good'. It is 'good' for the country because it exports a lot, and helps pay for our everyday needs. Thirdly, noise is 'bad'. So somehow we have to work towards the elimination of noise while encouraging the growth of air transportation and aircraft building industry. Those are the grounds on which I stand.

But how could we possibly eliminate the noise problem? The first obvious way might be to scrap the noisy aircraft and replace them with new quiet types. The airlines would not like that because it costs a lot of money. But if the government were to meet the costs because we all hate noise, the flying industry would like it, the builders would like it, and the population would like it because the noise problem was overcome but hate it because the costs are altogether too horrifically high.

Let me quantify this by saying that the biggest noise is made by the 707-type of aeroplane. I mean the VC10s, the DC8s, the 707 and its variants. There are approximately 1,400 of these aeroplanes and more are being built – with an expected life of 20 years. One of them makes as much noise on takeoff as all the world's population shouting at once, or equivalent to 20,000 motor cycles! There is no point in curing the noise of future aircraft while one allows the 1,400 big noise-producing kind to fly. The problem of aircraft noise is not the design and construction of a *new* quiet aeroplane; it is the elimination of the noisy ones, which have been built at a cost of around £5 million each to work for 20 to 25 years. The rules under which they have been bought allow them to be operated and any major abrupt change to those rules might lead to a catastrophic bankruptcy in the airline industry. One cannot rationally contemplate this situation.

Present choices and costs

I estimate that most of the 707-types are about half-way through their life and are probably worth about a million pounds apiece. So the investment in the 707-type fleet is of the order of £1,000 million pounds, which is about the cost of building Maplin. If the sole reason for building Maplin were to relieve the aircraft noise nuisance, I would consider scrapping the existing large jet fleet and its replacement by new aircraft as a far more effective measure for the same order of cost. The reason is that they could be replaced by much quieter aircraft from which everybody would gain. But I think that is most unlikely to happen.

If we now consider the makers of annoyance, as opposed to the makers of noise, the type of aircraft is slightly different because the smaller aircraft use the airports more frequently than the large long-range jets. These are the 727s, the Tridents, the BAC-111, the DC9-type of aeroplane, all engined by the Spey class of engine, which cause by far the most annoyance at the major airports. What can we do about them? There is not available on the shelf an aircraft which would be 10 or 20 decibels quieter. The problem is therefore different from that of the larger jets. As we have seen, they could in principle be replaced by the 747, which is 10 decibels quieter, or by long-range DC10s or Tristars, which would be 20 decibels quieter. It is simply a question of economics whether we think this is worthwhile or not.

With the smaller aircraft this option is not yet available. Alternatives have still to be generated, but the technology is available. The Spey engine derives a large part of its thrust by exhausting at high velocity air that has passed through the main combustion system. The big advance in technology that has allowed the large wide-bodied aircraft to operate at such low noise levels is to by-pass most of the flow going into the front through a huge fan so that it does not get heated and does not come out at very high speed. The Spey is a generation earlier, but the technology that is known to cure the noise problem of the large wide-bodied jets could be applied to the Spey, if fitted with a bigger fan. That is known to be technically possible. It would cost between £20 and £40 million to develop a new fan, and it might cost £20 to £40 million to modify the aeroplane to take the modified engine. But having got it, we would have an engine that is much quieter, more economical, with a higher thrust. And the airlines would welcome it. But the system is not available. It may become available but at the moment it is difficult to see who is going to provide the initiative for spending something like £60 million to manufacture an engine simply because it is quieter.

As long as there is no law against making noise, what is the incentive for the manufacture of a quieter engine? I see no immediate answer, although I believe lack of noise will pay in the future. It is difficult to see at present any incentive for manufacturing an aircraft that is quieter than existing types if this achievement is going to cost money. The research into aircraft noise is financed through the Department of Trade and Industry, charged with seeing that the industry is healthy. The measurement of health is its profitability, not its production of socially desirable products.

The technology is available for making the smaller type of aircraft distinctly quieter but the product is not yet in the development stage. I would estimate that some 4,000 of these aircraft exist, and if the re-fanned Spey type of engine were available it would presumably be introduced into the aeroplane as the used engines are replaced. If an aircraft requires several sets of engines in its life, there would not be the cost of scrapping the old engines. On a time-scale of, say, five years with a development cost of the order of £60 million, I cannot see why we should not expect to get ten decibels off the noise level of the bigger producers of annoyance.[1]

[1]'Note on Decibels', p. 38.

Silencing devices

Aircraft today have a life of approximately 20 years. Even though we can foresee that when they die the aircraft that will naturally replace them will be quieter by as much as 20 decibels, an enormous improvement, they may not be quiet enough. Further continuing research is needed to improve the position.

In the shorter term one can conceive of fitting a device to the noisy aircraft to lower the noise. Such devices, known as 'hush kits' or 'retrofit kits', are designed to take away some of the annoying noise. There are two elements to the noise of large jets, one generated by the jet as it mixes with its surroundings at very high speed, and the other made by the machinery that creates the jet. The machinery noise is generated within a shroud and can be absorbed by fitting acoustic liners. It can thus be reduced very dramatically: 10 or 20 decibels is quite readily achieved. But fitting liners costs money and the weight of a liner somewhat impairs the aircraft performance. The manufacture and fitting of a liner increases the operating costs and that has to be paid for. This 'retrofit' question is different from the options I discussed earlier where quiet new technology engines improved aircraft performance. With 'retrofit' or 'hush-kit', the kit goes on purely as a silencing device, and has to be paid for throughout the life of the aircraft as it costs more to run.

There is also the jet noise which is much more difficult to tackle. No technology is yet available which would guarantee a reduction of 10 decibels in the noise of a jet. Consequently, it is difficult to think of a way of bringing about a significant reduction in noise at take-off. I think this makes the whole 'retrofit' option rather doubtful. Even though we could bring about large reductions in the landing noise, we cannot really affect the take-off significantly.

Maplin no answer

But how do these considerations affect Maplin? They probably do not very much, except that if the main reason for building Maplin is the hope that it would remove the noise problem from Heathrow, the assumption is quite simply wrong. If that is the argument, the public should be informed that there are more effective ways of spending £1,000 million to reduce noise. The worry I have is that once sums are committed on this scale, in the interest of the environment to stop noise, it might be a retrogressive step. The reason is that it would then be extremely difficult to justify further increases in expenditure for a general attack on the noise problem which would be effective for all time and everywhere, and not only at London.

A NOTE ON DECIBELS

The ear responds to pressure, and the difference in levels between the minimum pressure that can be heard and the pressure which causes pain is very large. To relate these large numbers on a more compact scale, a logarithm is taken and the logarithmic sound level is called the 'decibel'. Ten decibels make a factor of ten, so that ten identical aircraft flying together make a noise ten decibels more than one. Twenty decibels is a factor of a hundred. If the noise level is reduced by twenty decibels, which is the difference between the 707-type of aircraft and the large wide-bodied jets, it takes a hundred of these new aircraft flying at once to make the same noise as one wide-bodied aircraft. That is a very substantial improvement. But I think it unlikely that the noise problem will be completely solved even with these wide-bodied aircraft.

The level of the general urban background noise is of the order of 75 decibels, and the level that we know to be achievable with current technology is of the order of 90 decibels. Such aircraft could still be heard and probably will still cause some annoyance. But they will be incomparably quieter than most aircraft today.

IV. *Alternatives to Maplin*

CHRISTOPHER FOSTER

Director, Centre for Urban Economics,
London School of Economics

IT SEEMS to me important to realise that the case against Maplin does not rest upon cost-benefit analysis issues, over which there is likely to be a difference of opinion among experts. It does not turn upon whether one accepts cost-benefit analysis as a technique, or whether one thinks it is or is not capable of being improved. Neither does it depend on tricky questions to do with such technical matters as the valuation of time.

The rational case against Maplin is now extremely robust. In relation to every issue – aviation, environmental, shipping, and (land) planning – there would seem to be an alternative which would secure at least the same benefit at substantially less cost.

This does not mean that one should not try to understand why a position was reached in which the Conservative Government was committed to Maplin. I would like to return to this question at the end.

It seems to be helpful to divide the issues into four: aviation, environmental, seaport and regional planning.

(1) *Aviation*

1. The Civil Aviation Authority has shown[1] that there is no shortage of runway capacity in the South-East until at least 1985. The Government accepted this view.[2]
2. The Civil Aviation Authority has also shown[3] – clearly in the first draft of their report, as certainly but more obscurely in the

---

[1]Civil Aviation Authority, *Forecasts of Air Traffic and Capacity at Airports in the London Area*, London, May 1973, paras. 7.17, 7.27, 10.9.

[2]*Hansard*, 8 May, 1973, col. 209.

[3]*Op. cit.* The most extensive extracts from the first draft were given in the *Guardian*, 21 April, 1973.

published report – that there need be no shortage of terminal capacity at Heathrow and Gatwick.

But the Conservative Government tried to suggest that it would cost almost as much to provide this capacity at Heathrow as it would at Maplin.

This must be nonsense. It will cost at least £825 million[4] to provide a two-runway airport at Maplin because of reclamation costs and access costs. Sir Peter Masefield tells me that at 'yesterday's prices' it would cost about £12 million to compensate the Greater London Council for the sludge works at Heathrow and about another £10 million to build the necessary terminal buildings.[5] Even if one were to double this to some £45 million or double it again to £90 million the cost is very small by comparison with providing similar terminal capacity at Maplin. I think at the very least one must challenge the Civil Aviation Authority to show how they can believe this untrue.

3. There is ample access capacity to Heathrow and Gatwick. The Piccadilly extension to Heathrow is already under construction. It should be sufficient. Even if it should become congested there are plans for a British Rail link from Victoria which has been costed and is far cheaper[6] than the completely new access required to Maplin. (Quite apart from all the social costs of building such road and rail links, which will be higher to Foulness than to Heathrow.)

Forecasting demand

Thus on aviation grounds the case for Maplin ceases to exist. The Conservative Government had a reserve argument. It posed the problem it thought would arise if the Civil Aviation Authority should have got its forecasts wrong. *First,* it is important to emphasise that even if the Civil Aviation Authority's highest forecasts were realised there will be spare capacity in 1985. We are therefore talking of growth rates higher than the Civil Aviation Authority's highest. *Second,* there have been improvements in forecasting. The original Department of Trade

---

[4]Mr Eldon Griffiths, *Hansard,* 13 June, 1973, col. 1,598–1,603. But see Sir Peter Masefield, 'The Road to Maplin', *Flight,* 16 August, 1973, p. 308.

[5]Private communications from Sir Peter Masefield, but see *ibid.,* p. 305.

[6]*Report of the Study of Rail Links with Heathrow Airport,* HMSO, 1970.

and Industry forecasts[7] were largely based on extrapolation. Obviously what has happened recently determines the future. The Civil Aviation Authority forecasts[8] represent a move towards behavioural analysis in which income, journey purpose, etc., become more important. The Channel Tunnel forecasts are better still.[9] They are wholly behavioural. They have been retrodicted to fit past events and they forecast substantially lower volumes of holiday traffic by air than do the Civil Aviation Authority. The main reason is easily explained. The major cost reduction effected some years ago by the package tour caused a rapid increase in the volume of holiday traffic by air and was the main factor explaining the acceleration in the increase of air traffic as a whole. Any forecasts based on trends will over-predict future growth unless it is reasonable to assume that there will continue to be developments similar to the introduction of the package tour and which will have the same effect in increasing air holiday traffic. This pitfall is avoided by forecasts based on behavioural analysis. Because both the Department of Trade and Industry and the Civil Aviation Authority forecasts gave too much weight to the continuation of these cost-reducing factors in the future, they were over-estimating demand particularly for holiday travel.

All this, however, is a digression to show that there is more reason behind the changing forecasts than may at first appear, and more reason to think that lower forecasts are more reliable. But it is irrelevant to the real point at issue, since even if the Government were correct in fearing that the growth of traffic might exceed the Civil Aviation Authority's highest forecast, it is no justification for building Maplin. We have five, some would say ten or fifteen, years to plan for the 1990s and beyond and to produce a contingency plan should the Civil Aviation Authority, the Channel Tunnel, etc., forecasts be wrong.

In drawing up such a plan the important factors are:

(1) economies in airport capacity that could be achieved by

---

[7]Department of Trade & Industry, *Working Party on Traffic and Capacity at Heathrow*, CAP 349, March 1971.

[8]*Op. cit.*

[9]*Channel Tunnel, Economic Report, Section 1, Passenger Studies: Main Report*, Coopers & Lybrand, 30 June, 1973.

airport pricing and other methods to secure better distribution of traffic through the day at airports;
(2) the contribution of regional airports in future;
(3) the contribution of the Channel Tunnel, particularly if high-speed trains should be feasible;
(4) the effect of developing the Advanced Passenger Train or other inter-city routes competitive with air; and
(5) in the more distant future the effects of RTOL aircraft or any other aircraft which will have less need for runway capacity than existing aircraft.

All these are relevant to the question that the Civil Aviation Authority and the Government ought to be asking: is there likely ever to be a need for a third London Airport? As a last fall-back there is the option of providing more runway capacity in the South-East, e.g. another runway at Stansted at a cost of some £10 million. This option is rightly ruled out under present conditions of aircraft noise but it ought, if absolutely necessary on traffic grounds, to be possible to provide some extra runway capacity, while maintaining the overriding constraint that aircraft noise *at all airports* should be progressively reduced over the next ten to twenty years. As stated in the Civil Aviation Authority report,[10] the 35 per cent increase in traffic they consider at Stansted and Luton could be associated with a very considerable reduction in noise below the present levels.

(2) *Environmental*
1. Few doubt that the environmental effect of building Maplin will be adverse, even disastrous, in South-East Essex, and likewise the effect of building the road and rail access routes to London.
2. The environmental case for Maplin is all to do with noise around Heathrow and Gatwick. I do not want to add to what Professor Ffowcs-Williams had to say, except to emphasise that the effect of building Maplin on present plans would be trivial compared with the reduction in noise from the introduction of quieter aircraft already in service.

What is needed here – and it must be the Government's job to work out a strategy – is some combination of introducing

[10]*Op. cit.*

existing aircraft more quickly, accelerating the introduction of new aircraft, *subsidising* the airlines to quieten existing aircraft with hush-kits, *subsidising* the aero-industry to invest in building much quieter engines, even engines producing no more than background noise. It will also have to negotiate with foreign governments and airlines in order to work out a mutually acceptable policy, so that foreign aircraft are not markedly noisier than domestic aircraft. Fortunately the countries with the largest international fleets are also most conscious of public opposition to noise. Airlines that persist in using noisy aeroplanes can expect to be required to use airports where their noise will have less environmental effects at times of day also when they may be expected to be less of a nuisance.

What are the other environmental arguments?

(1) One can see why people now suffering from aircraft noise around airports in the South-East are not easily persuaded out of their instinct that the building of Maplin will relieve their suffering. They are right that there will be a relatively small additional benefit to them purchased at high cost to others. If the Government shows no sign of developing a more rational policy which will bring them more benefits in terms of relief from noise at less cost, their attitude is justified.

(2) Only by largely closing down Heathrow would substantial relief be obtained from Maplin. This cannot happen – and the Government has never argued the case – because it would imply a much larger city in South-East Essex than the Government has promised and which it is possible to construct in a reasonable time. In exchanges the Roskill Commission mentioned a range of 230,000 – 270,000 as the population of such a city, as did the report of the South-East Essex Joint Planning Team. Essex County Council has always insisted that 250,000 was the maximum that it was ready to tolerate on environmental grounds. It was therefore something of a shock to find Mr Rippon's consultative document envisaging a growth of 300,000.[11] Closing down Heathrow would imply a much larger city – probably of

[11]Third London Airport Commission, *Report*, HMSO, 1971; *Strategic Plan for the South East*, South East Joint Planning Team, HMSO, 1970; *Maplin Project: New Town Designation Area*, Department of the Environment, Consultative Document, Rt. Hon. Geoffrey Rippon, 23 July, 1973.

the order of 500,000 – much larger than most regard as the maximum tolerable on environmental grounds. But it is difficult to foresee growth on this scale being practical for another reason. 5,000 persons per annum is a substantially higher rate of growth than any new town has achieved; and there is no one who can confidently promise a higher rate. It would therefore seem likely to take at least 50 years to build up to a population of 250,000 while by the mid-eighties it will be remarkable to have achieved a population of 50,000 (which itself throws doubt on the possibility of manning and servicing the airport at Maplin by then).

Nor must one forget that the closing down of Heathrow would have a very serious economic effect upon the surrounding area which – presumably because of the airport – has been *one of the few* areas of employment growth within London during the 1960s. It would not be surprising if the protests of people affected by closing the airport were at least as large as the protests of those now affected by noise from it. Transferring airport-related jobs and people from around Heathrow to South-East Essex would in itself be a complex and costly operation even if it were possible to provide a large enough city in Essex for all this activity. Thus even if it were feasible – which it is not – the effective costs, both direct and social, of closing down Heathrow and transferring its activities to Maplin would be very large.

(3) *The Seaport*

1. The Conservative Government conceded that the seaport would not be usable without the airport. This ought to dispose of the case for the seaport; it probably will not. Indeed, it is said that some of the reclamation costs attributed to the airport are properly attributable to the seaport, since if there were no seaport the reclamation costs would not have to be so high. It is also rumoured that the seaport will not be viable even if all the reclamation and access costs were borne by the airport. Until the PLA or NPC publish the costs and expected returns from the proposal one cannot know if these suggestions are true.

2. Is there a case for an oil and container port at Maplin? The National Ports Council has not given its opinion, though as

[44]

statutory adviser to the Government on port policy and port investment it might have been expected to do so. Because dredging and reclamation costs are high, because large oil tankers in particular would find it difficult to enter the Thames to approach Maplin, and generally because of congestion in the Channel, the case for an oil and container port at Maplin does not seem strong. I suspect the case for Maplin is mainly an understandable move by the PLA to remain a major authority as its older docks in the Pool of London close down. If there is a case for another container port, or more container berths, on cost grounds one would expect to find them at Southampton, as Sir Humphrey Browne, the Chairman of the British Transport Docks Board, has suggested,[12] or possibly at Hull or on Teesside. On regional grounds, all three have a better claim than London, with Hull and Teesside having more to offer than Southampton.

3. The notion that Maplin might become a British Rotterdam has no more to commend it. If this prospect means a major industrial complex located at a port, then on regional grounds Hull or Teesside would have a far better claim, as indeed would the Mersey. If it means another Europort, now that Rotterdam is congested and difficult to enlarge, this can hardly be anywhere else than on the continent of Europe, probably at Antwerp which is already growing fast. Large-scale transshipment of freight across the North Sea from Maplin must raise costs. In any case, anything approaching a Rotterdam is quite impossible at Maplin for exactly the same reason as it is impossible to close down Heathrow and transfer all its traffic there. The size of the city implied by even a small-scale Rotterdam breaks the promises given limiting new urbanisation in the area to 350,000.

(4) The Regional Planning Argument

1. Many authorities in regional planning would argue that it is no longer true, as it seemed to be even five years ago, that there is an almost desperate search for new housing in the South-East for London overspill and natural growth in population elsewhere. Rather the prospect is that we have too many new and expanded towns for the population of the South-East.

[12]Reported in *The Times,* 12 June, 1973.

This in itself is not an argument for not going ahead with the new city of Maplin since one could cut back in expansion elsewhere. But if the air and seaport are not built it is difficult to think of a good reason for building a new town at Maplin, and there are several reasons against doing so, notably the poor access from South-East Essex to the rest of the country and the closeness of the proposed new town development to Southend.

2. The case is often argued as if something needed to be done to give as many opportunities for the dispersion of jobs and homes to the East of London as to the West, with the implication that this could be an argument for proceeding with the new town at Maplin. That there has been a tendency for new and expanded towns to develop to the North-West and South of London rather than to the North-East is an unsurprising result of the geographical location of London. But lack of geographical symmetry is not in itself a rational argument. An argument that could be used is that there is a tendency for both jobs and people to move out along a radius starting from the centre of London, so that those to the North-West move out in that direction, those to the North-East, to the North-East; and so on. Thus it might be argued that there are fewer opportunities for jobs and people wishing to disperse from the East End of London if it is in practice true that they would wish to move along such a radius. The fallacy here is surely that there are a number of new towns and expanded towns to the North of the East End of London and that people from there do move to them. It is difficult to argue that there are not sufficient relocation possibilities for workplaces and people in the East End.

3. It is often argued as if Maplin would help Dockland. Experience suggests that Maplin is much too far away from Dockland to stimulate any substantial employment there even if the access routes were to go through the Dockland area (which they are not). One would have imagined that far more relevant to the revival of Dockland is the location of the London terminal of the rail approaches to the Channel Tunnel.

Conclusion

Thus, it is hard to discover a substantial argument in favour of Maplin which could possibly justify such a large expenditure.

[46]

What is required, it would seem, is a number of factual and policy papers.

1. We need a costing of the terminal capacity at Heathrow and Gatwick if used for the additional traffic the Civil Aviation Authority suggests.

2. Contingency plans should be proposed against the possibility that the highest Civil Aviation Authority forecasts are exceeded. The alternative policies to be considered are:

(i)   airport pricing[13] and other methods of increasing the efficiency of use of existing airports;

(ii) possible more use of regional airports;

(iii) the effect of the Channel Tunnel upon the use of airports and the further effect if speeds are increased by the Advanced Passenger Train;

(iv) the effect on air services from the South-East of Advanced Passenger Trains on other routes;

(v)   the feasibility of RTOL or other similar innovations on the long-run demand for runway capacity.

3. A proposal should be drawn up to set noise reduction targets on a year-by-year basis at every airport. The strategies to be considered include:

(i)   accelerated introduction of existing quieter aircraft;

(ii) accelerated introduction of even quieter new aircraft;

(iii) fitting 'hush-kits' to existing aircraft; and

(iv) a research programme for exploring the feasibility of still quieter engines whose noise levels may be no higher than ambient noise. It should also be possible to introduce stricter controls forcing noisy aircraft to use particular airports at particular times.

Many of these actions will require subsidy, but the cost-effectiveness of such subsidies in reducing aircraft noise would be more than building Maplin. International action is needed to persuade major airlines to co-operate. Environmental concern in many countries means it should not be politically impossible. If major countries and major airlines agree to adopt a quieter aircraft policy, it would be politically easy to impose restrictions on the remaining noisy aircraft.

[13]I. M. D. Little and K. M. McCleod, 'The New Pricing Policy of BAA', *Journal of Transport Economics & Policy*, May 1972.

4. A seaport plan should explore not only the commercial and financial feasibility of Maplin but also compare with alternative developments elsewhere.

5. A new policy is required on new and expanded towns in the South-East. Given that the major problem of the South-East is no longer the search for more sites for new and expanded towns, but rather spare capacity, the South-East plan should be revised to take in new priorities.

To make sure that these policies are formulated and published, it would be sensible to move a clause amending the Maplin Bill on the following lines (shorn of legal jargon):

'The Secretary of State for the Environment shall consult with the following bodies:
Civil Aviation Authority
National Ports Council
British Airways Board
British Airports Authority
Noise Advisory Council.
He shall also publish detailed proposals on road and rail access routes from the airport and seaport, and then publish a White Paper presenting the views of those bodies on the demand for the airport or seaport, as relevant in each case, on alternative strategies to the proposed airport and seaport, terminal capacity, contingency plans, environmental or noise reduction plans, seaport plans, plans for the South-East, and draw conclusions on the results of these consultations. This White Paper shall be debated in both Houses of Parliament before starting any reclamation, dredging or construction for either seaport or airport.'

Although there is still opportunity to insert a stronger clause when the Bill returns to the Commons, the House of Lords has unfortunately accepted a weaker form of words which does not require the government to report the views of the various bodies but only to consult them, and make its own re-assessment. With such a history of political pressures brought to bear, one wonders whether the government will produce the rational re-assessment which would surely inevitably question the wisdom of continuing with the project.

When there is so little that is rational to be said in favour of a project of this scale, it seems extraordinary that it should be proceeded with. If Maplin is not stopped the price paid for administrative inertia or *'politics'* (or political obstinacy) – whichever it is – is stupendously high. One fears that the traditional checks and balances – the role of the Treasury in approving major public expenditures, the role of the Cabinet which normally, as in this case, has had to approve the project, as well as scrutiny by both Houses of Parliament – have failed to perform their function. If they fail in a case such as this, we should not expect to find them more effective in stopping other projects which may be smaller but in some cases could be equally, if not at the present equally demonstrably, wasteful. If Maplin is built, one consequence should be an overhaul of our traditional and constitutional safeguards against the waste of public funds.

V. Summing Up and Verdict
SIR PETER MASEFIELD

SINCE THE initial decision of the Conservative Government to choose Foulness – now Maplin – as the site for a new third London airport (against the majority recommendation of the Roskill Commission), two further major changes have occurred. First, during the Commons debate on the third reading of the Maplin Development Bill on 23 October, 1973, the then Conservative Government gave an assurance that before major expenditure was authorised or incurred at Maplin, it would report to Parliament on a detailed study for consideration and debate. It would review the forecasts of air traffic up to 1990, examine the use of regional airports and the likely effects of the Channel Tunnel, examine ground-handling capacities at existing airports and the effects of aircraft noise in which, as Mr Michael Heseltine said, 'substantial progress is being made'. Secondly, the new Labour Government which came to office in March 1974 decided upon a further and complete re-assessment of the situation and that, ahead of it, no expenditure should be incurred on the Maplin project.

Major advance
This is a major step forward towards what Professor Heath has described as the essential

> 'taking account of both the political realities of the situation and of the management problems under conditions of uncertainty'. (p.16)

One may hope that the promised new examination of all the factors will go some way, also, towards satisfying Mr Foster's stricture that so large an expenditure must be the subject of a proper scrutiny and assessment by 'our traditional and constitutional safeguards against the waste of public funds' – in which the Treasury, the Cabinet and both Houses of Parliament should play their 'watchdog' roles.

During the second half of 1973, uncertainties have become sharper not only about the ultimate costs of Maplin in an inflationary spiral but also about the number of transport movements to pay for it. The cost has risen and the apparent demand has fallen.

Uncertainty and rapid change

In view of such uncertainties it is more than ever desirable to keep open all available options: to avoid premature commitments to massive capital spending which would lead at the same time to irreversible environmental changes.

Since the Roskill Commission Report in January 1971, the situation has been radically modified by advances in technology, by inflation, by increased fuel prices, by fuel shortages, and by the potentialities of the Channel Tunnel. In new circumstances, it would be economically disastrous and politically inept to attempt to solve tomorrow's problems by building yesterday's airport. In aviation, where technology marches fast, yesterday's problems smack of the Stone Age. They have little relevance to tomorrow's problems.

There is, of course, force in the argument that contingency plans should be made to meet possible long-term requirements for additional runway capacity if some of the current uncertainties in technological development, and in traffic growth, should eventually result in a demand for additional facilities. But an objective analysis of all the evidence does not suggest that, in today's circumstances, a case has been made for the commitment of large sums to Maplin now – or, indeed, that it is the best coastal site available if and when new runway capacity is required.

Five major changes since Roskill

Five major changes in relevant factors have occurred since the Roskill Commission reported – changes which sharpened in the last months of 1973. They are:

> *increases* in aircraft load capacities;
> *reductions* in noise;
> *increases* in potential runway capacities;

[51]

long-term reductions in transport aircraft frequencies – through fuel problems and costs;

potential cut-backs in the growth of short-haul air traffic.

1. *Aircraft size*

The average capacity of transport aircraft flying through the chief airports has increased much more than was forecast. At Heathrow the 'actuals' have gone up from an average of 52 passengers per flight in 1963 to 77 in 1973, or by 48 per cent. The trend is accelerating as new aircraft on order are delivered. The average now seems likely to reach about 180 passengers an aircraft by 1985 (taking all the London airports together) compared with the Roskill forecast of 162. That means that the same number of aircraft movements in the London area would by then accommodate an additional 10 million passengers.

2. *Noise*

Average noise levels around the chief airports have now passed their peaks and have begun to fall, partly through night restrictions and partly because new, quieter aircraft are beginning to comprise a significant proportion of the total movements. Around Heathrow the 90 PNdB footprint[1] covers about 60 square miles. By 1980 that area of disturbance is likely to be halved for some 90 per cent of the movements. By 1983 it could be brought down to an area of no more than about six square miles – one-tenth of the present area – for the mass of aircraft movements. That would represent a dramatic reduction in the level of disturbance and in the number of people affected – *without* Maplin. *With* Maplin it would remain about the same.

3. *Runway capacity*

Improved techniques of air traffic control, improved aircraft performance, the spreading of peaks and 'Mixed Mode' operations on parallel runways (as at Heathrow) can now increase the available, and safe, capacity of existing runways substantially, even taking account of wake turbulence. Heathrow's potential annual capacity can now, for instance, be seen as around 340,000

[1]PNdB means perceived noise level in decibels (dB): on this scale 90 PNdB is regarded as obtrusive.

transport aircraft movements compared with Roskill's forecast of 327,000. That is 13,000 more movements, roughly equivalent to an additional 2.4 million passengers a year by 1985 – or 3.4 million extra by 1995.

4. *Fuel problems*

Long-term shortages and soaring prices of aviation fuels are reducing the frequency of scheduled air services on trunk routes. The long-term result will be more emphasis on still larger aircraft to carry more passengers and cargo in fewer frequencies. For the first time since Heathrow opened in 1946 the transport aircraft movements in 1975 appear likely to be fewer than those in the previous years. As a result the approach towards runway saturation will be further delayed.

5. *Short-haul services*

The Channel Tunnel and the Advanced Passenger Train for high density short-haul services (both cross-Channel and domestic), together with the aviation fuel problems, seem likely significantly to reduce the rate of growth of high-cost, short-haul air services compared with the forecasts made at the time of Roskill.

All this, plus more direct services from provincial cities, indicates a trend under which existing airports will continue to be able to cope with air traffic demands for an indefinite period – subject to two important limitations: terminal capacity and ground access. Air traffic will increasingly be carried in smaller numbers of quieter, much larger aircraft. With Reduced Take-Off and Landing aircraft (RTOL) in the future, the possibilities of still more effective and economic use of existing airports at further reduced levels of exterior disturbance are now brighter than they have been since the jets came into service some 20 years ago.

Expansion of airport capacity

More terminal capacity at existing airports and better access will, however, be required urgently. But these *can* be provided economically.

The Perry Oaks area within the Heathrow boundaries, between the main runways to the west of the central area, is at present – inappropriately – occupied by a sewage sludge works made up of drying beds. By a redeployment of this sludge works – first proposed in 1943 – the available apron and terminal space at Heathrow could be more than doubled. Such action is required well before 1982 anyway to cope more comfortably and conveniently with the existing traffic. A Perry Oaks development could be designed, alongside existing amenities, to extend the capacity of the airport (at substantially lower levels of disturbance) to around 90 million passengers a year with modern facilities – eliminating long walks. An example of what can be done, to high standards, is Newark, the oldest New York airport, which has recently undergone a 'face-lift' to bring it to a standard well up to the best in 1974. There is room within the present boundaries of Heathrow, Gatwick and Stansted to do the same at a cost-effectiveness which is much higher than that at Maplin.

And that goes for surface access, too. The improvement of the M.4 and the completion of M.3, M.11, M.23 and M.25 plus a direct Victoria-Feltham-Heathrow rail link (in addition to the LTE Underground) would reduce congestion and improve access times, as well as confer wider community benefits – without the environmental upheavals of a swathe through Essex to a dead-end airport.

In times of exceptional scarcity of fuel there is, more than ever, a case against the development of a remote airport. Not only are the air distances to and from Maplin longer for most destinations than for existing airports; the surface journeys for passengers and cargo are also much longer – by more than 50 per cent.

The cost, upheaval and environmental damage caused by Maplin could not be justified until it was handling at least 50 million passengers a year (and perhaps not even then). The surface journeys of 50 million passengers a year, each travelling an average of 25 extra miles to Maplin (a minimum) would amount to 1,250 million extra unnecessary and costly passenger-miles a year. At the very least 20 million extra and unnecessary gallons of fuel would be consumed each year on the surface alone – plus a similar additional amount in the air.

On the incidence of capital expenditure, Ministers have said the airport would be designed to be opened in 1982, and the cost would be of the order of £380 million, including access – but expenditure would be small up to 1977. That implies a very heavy expenditure indeed during the four years 1978 to 1981, possibly around £80 million a year, absorbing resources which can ill be spared, if at all.

Much of the case for additional capacity at Maplin rests on the argument for closing the runways at Stansted, Luton and Southend. Once the noise problem around existing airports has been solved – as it largely can be by the time Maplin could be fully operational in the middle 1980s – the case for closing Stansted, Luton and Southend evaporates. The powerful reasons against closure are spreading the load, travel convenience, and the economic use of resources, including human, which would have to be replaced at much higher costs.

The two fundamental questions are:

1. Would Maplin be a good and satisfactory airport to fulfil the uses for which it is intended?
2. Is it required within the foreseeable future?

An objective answer to both questions would appear to be 'No'.

The distance of Maplin from its traffic catchment-areas, its enormous relative costs, its location, and its environmental effects on a quiet and unspoiled area combine to justify the 'White Elephant' label attached to it by every aviation interest concerned.

Nor does the requirement for it exist in the changed circumstances since Roskill began work (pp. 51ff). Maplin would not significantly reduce noise around Heathrow and Gatwick where the surface congestion can be relieved by imaginative plans.

As Mr Foster has said (pp. 39–40):

'The Civil Aviation Authority has shown that there is no shortage of runway capacity in the South-East until at least 1985. The Government has accepted this view ... [and] that there need be no shortage of terminal capacity at Heathrow and Gatwick.'

Later evidence has pushed the 'at least 1985' projection into the more distant future.

A positive policy

There is no future in a negative policy. What is required is a plan for handling air traffic in the London area with maximum convenience and effectiveness, at low disturbance levels, at minimum cost, and at a high level of access and interchange-ability between the relevant forms of transport.

The evidence and forecasts suggest these objectives could be served by a 'Three Point Plan':

1. *A Strategic Noise Policy* under which increasingly stringent noise limitations would be imposed on aircraft using the London airports. For example, by 1979, CAR Part 36 requirements[1] would not only have to be met but also improved upon to the extent that no aircraft, whatever its weight, would be permitted to exceed a combination of Take-Off, Sideline and Approach EPNdB noise-level of 300 – half the disturbance level of the Boeing 707 and the DC-8. The one exception might have to be the Concorde with a limitation on the number and times of take-offs and landings. Nonetheless the Concorde by 1979 ought to be within CAR Part 36 limitations. By 1982 the total 'noise footprints' could be limited to a small percentage of those today.

2. *Additional Terminal Capacity* at existing airports broadly within their present boundaries. That would bring Perry Oaks into the Heathrow terminal area, together with terminal capacity north of the present runway at Gatwick and north-west of the runway at Stansted. There is no truth in the suggestion that such a terminal expansion is not practicable or economic – it can be both.

3. *Improved Access* in developed roads and rail services to Heathrow, Gatwick and Stansted along existing agreed lines.

Recent experience within the New York area has shown what can be achieved with a minimum of upheaval and a maximum of convenience from better use of locations. Such a policy would have the major merit of keeping open long-term options and

[1]The limits set in the United States for all newly-certified aircraft to define noise levels against aircraft weights.

yielding the maximum advantage from technical developments – notably in larger, quieter, reduced take-off and landing (RQTOL) aircraft and the Channel Tunnel – and the long-term effects of fuel shortages and higher prices.

It would make possible also the further review clearly required of the South-East Regional Plan which was based on a population of 17 million in 1966, and a forecast of 20 million for 1991 – now reduced to only 18.5 million (at half the rate of growth) with a different distribution (including South Essex up to the original forecast), a situation which would be further distorted by Maplin. More time is needed to examine these developments.

Summary

To sum up: new evidence since the Roskill Report – which did not favour Maplin – has further emphasised the high costs and low benefits of the proposal. Without Maplin, money would be liberated to improve the environment around existing airports to substantial advantage – compared with the harmful effects of imposing an airport and long access routes on an unspoiled countryside and coastline. Funds liberated for a concentrated attack on aircraft noise at source, under Section 8 of the Industry Act, 1972 (combined with an increasingly strict noise limitation policy) could bring down the average noise-scale by some 20 PNdB by the time Maplin could be in service. At that level not only would the noise footprint area be substantially reduced but 100 of the quieter aircraft flying together would create no more noise than one of today's noisier types.

Maplin would not, therefore, show a noise benefit compared with alternative solutions. The important task now is to identify objectively the alternative possibilities on rational – not emotional – arguments about the economic environment.

On today's evidence it seems clear that there is no case for Maplin on aviation grounds, as a 'reliever of noise' around existing airports, on economic or congestion grounds. There is a strong case against Maplin on regional planning, on countryside environmental, and on fuel conservation grounds. There is a strong case for a sound – and environmentally progressive – improvement of existing airports to meet the traffic requirements, and for a development of regional airports in line with growing and changing public demand.

The most powerful case of all is to keep the options open in a time of swift technological and economic change. The commitment of scarce resources to a project about which there must remain so many incontrovertible doubts, and which would cause so many irreversible changes to the countryside and the coastline, would seem to be neither well-founded nor wise in an unenlightened world.

IEA Publications

Subscription Service

An annual subscription to the IEA ensures that all regular publications are sent without further charge immediately on publication—representing a substantial saving.

The cost (including postage) is £10.00 for twelve months (£9.50 if by Banker's Order) – £7.50 for teachers and students; US $25 or equivalent for overseas subscriptions.

To: The Treasurer,
      Institute of Economic Affairs,
      2 Lord North Street,
      Westminster,
      London SW1P 3LB

Please register a subscription of £10.00 (£7.50 for teachers and bona fide students) for the twelve months beginning.............................

☐ Remittance enclosed   ☐ Please send invoice

☐ I should prefer to pay by Banker's Order which reduces the subscription to £9.50.

Name ....

Address ....

          ....

          ....

Signed ....

Date ....

OP40

IEA OCCASIONAL PAPERS in print

EATON PAPERS in print